Kids First!

Family Education Program

> Kids First™ is an organization committed to helping the world's most precious resource: our children. Our children's future starts with involved parents and a good education—neither of which can function alone.

Jennifer Burton Bauer, M.A.

Building our children's future together!

Kids First™

Family Education Program

Published by:

BLUE BIRD PUBLISHING

2266 S. Dobson, Suite #275
Mesa AZ 85202
(602) 831-6063
FAX (602) 831-1829
Email: bluebird@bluebird1.com
Web site: http://www.bluebird1.com

© 1997 by Jennifer Burton Bauer

ISBN 0-933025-59-9
$12.95

Children's IQ's and intelligence have very little to do with how well they do in school. It's really not a matter of how smart children are but how smart they study.

Learning study skills will help your children improve their grades. Students with average ability that do poorly in school do so only because nobody has taught them valuable study skills.

Unfortunately, many schools don't have the time to teach these skills. It is therefore, important for parents to be educated in these techniques and pass them on to their children.

Table of Contents

How to be a Better Role Model
7-Step Plan to Turning Your Home into a Learning
Environment
Parent and Child Contracts
Parenting Pledge
Checklist: Is Your Home Conducive to Learning?

Expectations
Goal Setting
Motivating Children
Building Self-Esteem

5-Step Homework Plan
Overcoming Roadblocks to Homework Success
Homework Pledge

Reading to Remember
Note-Taking and Mapping
Listening and Memory Skills
Music and Studying
Test Taking Skills

Table of
Contents

How To Use This Book

How To Use
This Book

Welcome to the Kids First!™ Family Education Program. You are about to make one of the best investments a parent can make: an investment in your children's future.

As a public school teacher for many years, I was often asked by parents what they could do to help their children succeed in school. I recommended books, seminars, and common sense tips.

Many parents, however, found they could not take time away from their families to read long involved books on how to teach math or English, or to attend seminars. They wanted a quick, easy-to-use resource guide to help them through their children's most formative years.

With today's family in mind, I developed the Kids First!™ Family Education Program. It is the first program of its kind that involves the whole family by providing parents with a self-study guide to help their children succeed in school.

The program is divided into 9 modules. Each module provides parents with tips, lists, and information for helping their children succeed in school. Activities in each module are designed to involve parents and children in enriching projects that promote school success.

The program allows parents to work through the book at their own pace or to use as an easy resource guide. Whatever your choice, it is the commitment to the education of our children that counts; a commitment to America's future.

The American Family is the rock on which a solid education can be built. I have seen examples all over this nation where two-parent families, single parents, stepparents, grandparents, aunts, and uncles are providing strong family support for their children to learn. If families teach the love of learning it can make all the difference in the world to their children.
Richard W. Riley

The first teachers are the parents, both by example and conversation. But don't think of it as teaching. Think of it as fun.
Lamar Alexander

Introduction

Introduction

How your children perceive themselves depends on their home environment. Learning does not start when the bell rings at school nor does it end when school lets out.

Schools, over the years, have been expected to take on the huge burden of educating our children. Yet, education is a partnership between parents and schools. True school reform begins with concerned and involved parents.

To create a stronger, safer, more enriching future for our children, parents must become partners in their children's education. This training manual will give you easy steps and fun ideas for being involved in your children's life and the world's future.

Consider these important facts:

● Three decades of research show that parental participation improves student learning.
● When parents expect their children to do well in

school, they do. Students who are encouraged by their parents to work hard in school are more likely to succeed in school than are children who are encouraged only by teachers or not encouraged at all.

- Children of families who get involved in education get better grades and test scores, graduate from high school at higher rates, are more likely to go on to higher education, are better behaved, and have more positive attitudes.

- Studies of individual families show that a families'attitude towards education plays a more important role in student success than family income or education.

- Family involvement is one of the best long-term investments a family can make. The difference in lifetime earning between a student who did not graduate from high school and one who did is over $200,000. The difference for a student who received a bachelor's degree or more is almost $1 million.

Introduction

**Module 1:
Home
Environment**

Parents who care about their children's education do the following:

1. Have high expectations.
2. View hard work as the key to success.
3. Use family time for home-centered learning activities.
4. Have clearly understood household rules that are consistently enforced.
5. Have frequent contact with teachers.
6. Have an active life.
7. Actively model and share a value for learning.

Module 1:
Home Environment

In this module you will learn:

● **How to be a better role model**
● **How to turn your home into a learning environment**
● **How to commit yourself to a partnership in your children's education**

11

Part 1
How to Be a Better Role Model

Module 1:
Home
Environment

Part 1
How to be a
better role model

Responsibility

You are your children's role model, whether you like it or not. Your children will most likely emulate what they see you doing. If you say that education is important, yet you don't show up to your children's conferences or support them in doing their homework then the message you are sending is that education is not very important. Therefore, it is important that you make an effort to be a good role model.

To be a good role model, parents must look at the following qualities:

R- Responsibility
O- Optimism
L- Leadership
E- Effort

Responsibility - It is your responsibility to see that your children get the best education possible. It would be wonderful if we could send our children off to school for six hours a day and have them return perfectly educated. Unfortunately, this is not the case. Parents need to become partners in their children's education.

Optimism- Your attitude and optimism about education will affect your children's view of education for the rest of their lives. Your actions and words about education strongly influence their attitude towards education. Even if you did not like school or graduate from high school or college, you should value education for your children's sake. Here are five reasons why you should be optimistic about your children's education:

1. You want them to succeed in a competitive world.
2. You care about their future.
3. You alone can make a significant impact on your children's education.
4. You know that with an education, your children's chances for success rise dramatically.
5. You want to make a difference in your children's lives.

   When your children see your positive attitude towards education then a positive attitude is going to be instilled in them. You can:

Module 1: Home Environment

Part 1 How to be a better role model

Optimism

Module 1:
Home
Environment

Part 1
How to be a
better role model

Leadership

Effort

1. Speak positively about education.
2. Use your actions to show you value education.
3. Become part of the solution rather than part of the problem.
4. Become a partner in your children's education.
5. Commit yourself to helping your children succeed in their education.

Leadership - Taking an active role in your children's education helps demonstrate leadership qualities. Research shows that parents make a difference by:

1. Offering encouragement to do well in school and praising success.
2. Taking an active interest by talking with their children about school.
3. Encouraging their children to ask questions and think independently.
4. Establishing a clear set of rules and expectations about acceptable behavior.
5. Emphasizing the importance of hard word and responsibility.

Effort - Anything worthwhile takes effort. It takes effort and commitment to become involved in your children's education. When you do the above mentioned things, you are sending a message to your children that education is important. That message will translate to a child who appreciates and respects the importance of succeeding in school.

> *You will never find time for anything...*
> *if you want time, you must make it.*
> Charles Buxton

Part 2
Turning Your Home
Into A Learning Environment

7-Step Plan For Turning Your Home Into A Learning Environment:

Step 1: Set aside ten minutes every day to talk with your children about their day at school.

Activity: Pick a convenient time of the day to talk

Module 1:
Home
Environment

Part 2
Turning
Your Home
Into A
Learning
Environment

7-Step Plan
For Turning
Your Home
Into A
Learning
Environment

Module 1:
Home
Environment

Part 2
Turning
Your Home
Into A
Learning
Environment

7-Step Plan
For Turning
Your Home
Into A
Learning
Environment

with your children about their school day. You may want to include other topics as well. For instance, current events, the day's weather, animals, good books to read, etc. Do this every day. Eventually it will become a habit.

Step 2: Set aside a specific study area for your children. This place should be quiet and free of distractions from the television, radio, other children, etc. The special spot should have a desk or table to work at, and a place to put school supplies.

Activity 1: Get together with your children and choose a special study spot. Ask your children where they will be most comfortable. Choose a place free from distractions and noise. This could be the kitchen table, a desk in the children's room, or a quiet spot in the den or living room of your house. If your children are in daycare and there is a quiet time provided, then you should work out with the daycare provider a special quiet place for your children to study in the afternoon.

Tell the children that this is their special study place. Then make signs with your children's names. Take a piece of cardboard and cover it with plain or wrapping paper using glue or tape. Have your children write on them "_____'s **Study Spot. Do Not Disturb!**" The sign can be used each day or evening when your children are studying.

Activity 2: Make a special box with study sup-plies for your children. Use a cardboard shoebox covered with paper, or buy a plastic storage box. The box should contain the following materials:

pencils	glue
erasers	tape
paper	ruler
scissors	dictionary
markers	stapler
pencil sharpener	

Step 3: Set aside a specific study time each day for your children. Consistency is the key. Children like routines and it will be reassuring to them and easier for you to manage if they have a specific study time everyday. The time should be convenient for the family, provide quiet time, and be consistent with your children's own natural internal schedules (some children work better at night, some first thing in the afternoon). Choose a time when an adult can super-vise.

   If your children do not have homework on a particular day or finish their work early, the time should be spent reading. A friend of mine with three children has a study time every evening after dinner from 7:00-8:00. The television is turned off and the kids do homework, study for tests, or read. She and

Module 1:
Home
Environment

Part 2
Turning
Your Home
Into A
Learning
Environment

7-Step Plan
For Turning
Your Home
Into A
Learning
Environment

Module 1:
Home
Environment

Part 2
Turning
Your Home
Into A
Learning
Environment

7-Step Plan
For Turning
Your Home
Into A
Learning
Environment

her husband use the time to read newspapers, magazines, or books, and are available to help the children if needed.

Activity: Choose a study time for your children. Use the chart below to determine the best time for your children based on their schedules. Consider the following when making the schedule:

1. Are there after school sports or activities that would prohibit a study time afterschool?
2. Are your children in a daycare situation? Do you want them to have their study time at daycare or at night when you can supervise them?
3. Will there be someone available to supervise the study time?
4. Is the time early enough in the evening so you will not be tired?

Time	Mon	Tues	Wed	Thurs	Fri
12:00					
1:00					
2:00					
3:00					
4:00					
5:00					
6:00					
7:00					
8:00					
9:00					

Step 5 - Become a model for reading. When you read and have an interest in books then it is more likely that your children will read and have an interest in books. Families should take time every night to read together. Magazines, books, and newspapers should be available in your home.

Activity: Take your children to the library and get library cards. Pick out a book for yourself and help your children find one. Then choose a time when the whole family can read together. After dinner is a good time for family reading time.

Step 6 - Limit television time. Consider these items when deciding how much television your children should watch each week:

1. Research indicates that the more time children spend watching TV, the lower their achievement scores; the less time they spend watching TV, the higher their scores.
2. Research indicates that more than ten hours of TV viewing time per week is considered detrimental to learning.
3. Teach your children how to use television creatively and critically.
4. Allow only certain hours and times for TV viewing, preferably after homework and chores are

Module 1: Home Environment

Part 2 Turning Your Home Into A Learning Environment

7-Step Plan For Turning Your Home Into A Learning Environment

completed.

5. At the beginning of each week, decide with your children which programs they can watch.

Module 1:
Home
Environment

Part 2
Turning
Your Home
Into A
Learning
Environment

7-Step Plan
For Turning
Your Home
Into A
Learning
Environment

Activity: Turn off the TV for an entire evening one night per week. Use the time to read together as a family, play games, talk about current events, or work on special projects.

Step 7- Plan leisure time activities that enhance learning. Learn to spend more time with your kids rather than money. With many parents both working, it is often easier to spend money rather than time with children. This, however, teaches children to value money instead of relationships.

Kids won't complain about not having the latest toy if they have parents who spend time with them and show them how to find joy in the simple things in life.

Activity: Use the list on the following page to help with ideas on leisure time activities to do with your children. Take the time to plan at least one educational leisure time activity a month.

> *If you want your children to turn out well, spend twice*
> *as much time with them, and half as much money.*
> Abigail "Dear Abby" Landers

10 Leisure Time Activities Families Can Do To Enhance Learning

1. Go to the zoo. Have your children ask questions beforehand about the animals they will see. Discuss the different habitats and adaptations of the animals, i.e., how polar bear's thick white fur enables them to blend into the white snow and keep them warm in the cold environment in which they live. Visit the library before your visit and research the animals you will be seeing. Do follow-up activities like making a book or doing research on a particular animal that really interested your children.
2. Go to museums. Museums of all types are available throughout the United States. Many museums specialize in hands-on children centers that expose children to a multitude of scientific concepts.
3. Go to planetariums. There are about 1,000 planetariums in the United States. Children can view the rings of Saturn through a telescope; see the "sky" from inside the planetarium's dome; and step on scales to learn what they would weigh on the moon or on Mars. To find the nearest planetarium call the astronomy or physics department at a local college, local science museum, or the science curriculum specialist in your school district.

Module 1:
Home
Environment

Part 2
Turning
Your Home
Into A
Learning
Environment

10 Leisure Time
Activities
Families
Can Do To
Enhance
Learning

Module 1:
Home
Environment

Part 2
Turning
Your Home
Into A
Learning
Environment

10 Leisure Time
Activities
Families
Can Do To
Enhance
Learning

4. Visit an aquarium. Aquariums enable children to learn first hand about ocean life. They are especially interesting at feeding time. Call ahead to find out the best times to visit.

5. If you live near the ocean, spend a day at the tidepools. Check with the local lifeguard station or newspaper to find out when low tide will be. Then get a book from the library on tidepools. Take a checklist of the animals and sea life you would like to find. Check it off as you view them.

6. Visit a farm. Call the closest 4-H club to find out where the closest farm is in your area. On a dairy farm, you will see cows, silos, and learn what cows eat. On a vegetable farm, your children will learn how various crops grow and the stages of development from growth to the supermarket.

7. Go on a nature hike. Observe different animals you see or look for larger animal prints. Talk about the different plants, flowers, and birds along the trail. Collect leaves or rocks.

8. Visit a botanical garden. Take a tour and discuss the various plants and habitats that you see.

9. Visit the library. Find out beforehand if there are any upcoming programs or story times that you can attend with your children.

10. Take your children to work with you for the day. Let them see what you do and take part in your career.

Part 3
Making the Commitment To Be A Partner In My Children's Education
Contracts for Parents and Children

Now's the time for both parents and children to commit themselves to being partners in education. Complete the following contracts and join in a committed partnership to the importance of a good education!

Contracts appear on the next two pages.

After completing the parent and child contracts, copy the parenting pledge and hang it where you will see it on a daily basis.

Module 1:
Home
Environment

Part 3
Making the
Commitment
To Be A
Partner
In My
Children's
Education

Parent Contract

1. I will take time out of my day to talk with my children about their education.
2. I will provide a home environment conducive to learning.
3. I will limit my children's TV time and be involved in what they choose to watch.
4. I will encourage my children to read and I will provide my children with reading materials in the home.
5. I will be a partner in my children's education because I know that I am my children's first teacher.
6. I will provide a specific study area and study time for my children to use every day or evening.
7. I will check my children's homework to be sure that assignments are completed.
8. I will attend parent conferences and communicate with teachers if I see problems in my children's homework.

Signed_____

Date_____

Child's Contract

1. I will talk to my parents about school every day.

2. I will do my homework every day or night at the time we agree upon. If I do not have homework, I will study for upcoming tests or quizzes, review, or read quietly.

3. I will talk to my parents if I am having problems at school.

4. I will work with my parents on my education and know that they are a partner to my educational process.

5. I will limit my TV time and choose to watch shows that are educational.

Signed_____

Date_____

Module 1:
Home
Environment

Part 3
Making the
Commitment
To Be A
Partner
In My
Children's
Education

Child
Colntract

25

Checklist: Is Your Home Conducive to Learning?

Go through this checklist every month. Note what things you are doing and what things you are not.

1. I talk to my children every day about their school day. _____
2. I have established clear expectations for my children in school. _____
3. I read regularly in front of my children. _____
4. Our family watches less than two hours of TV per day. _____
5. I monitor what my children watch on TV. _____
6. I subscribe to newspapers, magazines, and other reading materials. ____
7. My children have a library card and use it regularly. _____
8. I show an enthusiasm for learning. _____
9. I have a specific time and place for my children to study and do homework every day or night. _____
10. I help and encourage my children to their best. _____
11. I try to assure that my children eat healthy foods. _____
12. I help and encourage my children to do their

homework. _____

13. I attend school functions. _____

14. I show an interest in my children's' schoolwork.

_____

15. I praise my children for their effort and achievement. _____

16. I read to my children or encourage them to read every day. _____

17. If my children are having difficulties in a certain area, I follow through to help them with the problem. _____

18. I play games with my children that are mentally challenging._____

19. I take my children to museums or to other educationally oriented activities._____

20. I talk with my children about their future and how education fits into that picture. _____

You have successfully completed Kids First!™ Module 1. You may now review this module and continue to module 2.

Module 1:
Home
Environment

Part 3
Making the
Commitment
To Be A
Partner
In My
Children's
Education

Checklist:
Is Your
Home
Conducive to
Learning?

**Module 2:
Expectations,
Goal Setting,
Motivation, &
Self-Esteem**

> *One can never consent to creep...*
> *when one feels the impulse to soar!*
> Helen Keller

Module 2:
Expectations,
Goal Setting,
Motivation, &
Self-Esteem

Module 2:
Expectations, Goal Setting, Motivation, and Self-Esteem

In this module you will:

- **Establish clear expectations of your children**
- **Set goals with your children**
- **Learn how to motivate your children to achieve their goals**
- **Learn how to build your children's self-esteem**

Part 1: Expectations

Module 2:
Expectations,
Goal Setting,
Motivation, &
Self-Esteem

Part 1
Expectations

Parents that expect a lot from their children will find that their children live up to those expectations. A Pennsylvania study of high school students indicates that the strongest influence on student's plans to attend college was their parent's attitude. An overwhelming majority of students whose parents wanted them to attend college planned to do so. It is not too early to start talking about college at the elementary school level.

Activity: Help define your expectations of your children by filling out the following survey. First, complete the parent expectations (make extra copies if you have more that one child or write them down on a separate piece of paper for each child). Then, sit down with your children individually and ask them what they expect from school. Help them fill out their section. Afterwards, explain your expectations of them. Finally, fill in the ways you are going to work together to achieve both of your expectations.

Three expectations I have of my child in school:

1. _____

2. _____

3. _____

Three things my child expects from school:

1. _____

2. _____

3. _____

Three ways we can work together to achieve these expectations:

1. _____

2. _____

3. _____

Module 2:
Expectations,
Goal Setting,
Motivation, &
Self-Esteem

Part 2
Goal Setting

Part 2:
Goal Setting

> *Whether you think you can or think you can't,*
> *you're right.*
> Henry Ford

Goal setting is a useful tool. Research shows that people who write down their goals often attain them. Use the expectations above as a springboard to discuss and write on the following page each of your children's academic goals. Then write the ways you can help them achieve these goals.

Use these goals to teach your children not to give up on projects that seem tough. All too often children want immediate satisfaction. Explain

31

that success comes to those who work hard for it. Work with them on their goals, and praise them when they achieve one.

Three academic goals my child has:

1. _____
2. _____
3. _____

Three ways my child can achieve these goals:

1. _____
2. _____
3. _____

Three ways I can help my child achieve his or her goals:

1. _____
2. _____
3. _____

Part 3:
Motivating Children

> *You gain strength, experience, and confidence by every experience where you really stop to look fear in the face...You must do the thing you cannot do.*
> Eleanor Roosevelt

Module 2:
Expectations,
Goal Setting,
Motivation, &
Self-Esteem

Part 3
Motivating
Children

Now that you have committed yourself to helping your children in school, how do you encourage and motivate them to do well?

It is important that children are taught at an early age that success doesn't always come easy, and that hard work leads to accomplishment. Talk to your children about the road to success. Help them find a hero whose life can be an example for them. Use entrepreneurs, athletes, politicians, and historical figures that have overcome adversity to teach that persistence and hard work lead to success.

For example, the following person's life illustrates that persistence is the key to success in life. Can you guess who it is?

This person:

● failed in business
● ran for state legislature and lost
● lost his job and wanted to go to law school but couldn't get in
● went into business again but went bankrupt

Module 2:
Expectations,
Goal Setting,
Motivation, &
Self-Esteem

Part 3
Motivating
Children

- ran for state legislature again and won
- tried to become speaker of the state legislature and was defeated
- sought to become an elector but was defeated
- ran for congress and lost
- ran for congress again and won
- ran for re-election to Congress and lost
- sought the job of land officer in his home state but was rejected
- ran for Senate of the United States but lost
- sought the vice-presidential nomination at his party's national convention but got less than 100 votes
- ran for U.S. Senate again and lost

Do you know who this is? Without persistence this man would never have become our sixteenth president—Abraham Lincoln.

Besides using role models, the following steps will help you motivate your children to do well in school.

> *The dictionary is the only place where success comes before work.*

12 Easy Ways Motivate Children to Learn:

1. From an early age show them that learning is fun by weaving interesting learning activities into everyday situations (see Module 9).
2. Teach your children to value learning by valuing it yourself.
3. Give children encouragement when they are having a difficult time.
4. Teach your children that effort is often more important than success.
5. Teach children that an "I will" is more important than an "IQ."
6. Encourage children to develop interests they enjoy, i.e., music, sports, science, writing, clubs, etc.
7. Engage your children in active learning activities. Provide opportunities in the home for experimenting, writing, play-acting, building, drawing, and explaining.
8. Realize that each child is unique and learns in his or her own way. Find out how your children learn best and help them learn in the way that is easiest for them (see Module 7).
9. Children develop self-confidence through struggle and by seeing the relationship between the learning process and its outcomes.
10. Model and celebrate effort in the pursuit of a

Module 2:
Expectations,
Goal Setting,
Motivation, &
Self-Esteem

Part 3
Motivating
Children

12 Easy Ways
To Motivate
Children
To Learn

Module 2:
Expectations,
Goal Setting,
Motivation, &
Self-Esteem

Part 3
Motivating
Children

Activities For
Motivating
Children

chosen goal. Children need to learn that trying hard and putting forth an effort are what will lead them to accomplishment.

11. Teach your children that making mistakes is a part of life and that the important thing is not the mistake but to learn from it.

12. Teach children that "a quitter never wins, and a winner never quits."

Activities For Motivating Children

Activity 1: Choose three people that are good role models for your children, i.e., Helen Keller, Martin Luther King, Abraham Lincoln, Henry Ford, etc. Get books at the library or bookstore on them, and read to your children about one person each night. Ask your children questions about how that person over-came obstacles in his or her life? How did that person succeed? What did that person value? Ask your children what they would do to do something well? Come up with strategies that they can use to succeed.

Activity 2: Make a treasure map with your children. You will need: old magazines, glue, scissors, and a plain sheet of paper. Have your children think of things they would like to accomplish. This can include getting good grades, succeeding in sports, music, art, or other special activities. Cut out pictures that show them succeeding in these areas. Have them keep the maps in a place where they will be able to look at them often. Eventually, with hard work and persistence these goals should become reality!

Part 4:
Building Self-Esteem

10 Ways To Increase Your Child's Self-Esteem:

1. Refrain from comparing children to siblings. Each child is unique and learns at his or her own pace.
2. Write your children notes telling them how proud you are of a job well done and put them in their lunch boxes from time to time.
3. Avoid criticizing your children when they don't meet your expectations.
4. Give your children one-on-one time every day.

Module 2:
Expectations,
Goal Setting,
Motivation, &
Self-Esteem

Part 4
Building
Self-Esteem

10 Ways
To Increase
Your Child's
Self-Esteem

Module 2:
Expectations,
Goal Setting,
Motivation, &
Self-Esteem

Part 4
Building
Self-Esteem

10 Ways
To Increase
Your Child's
Self-Esteem

Even it's just five minutes talking to them before bed time.

5. Give your children at least one hug every day.

6. Give your children responsibilities.

7. Tell your children one nice thing you like about them everyday.

8. What your say about your children in front of other people will affect their self-concept. If you want them to feel good about themselves say positive things about them.

9. Instead of nagging at your children to do things, use humor to get them to do chores, homework, etc. Leave notes like ***The Health Department will be inspecting this room at 2:00 tomorrow afternoon*** or ***The Homework Fairy will be leaving a treat for those who get their homework done before 5:00 without complaining.***

10. Children love to hear praise. Give praise when it is deserved. When praising children be specific, and tell them exactly what they did that you thought was good. What follows are some phrases of encouragement you can use.

Phrases to use when giving praise:

Good job!   *Great Effort!*

I knew you could do it!   *I'm proud of you!*

That's great!   *Nice try!*

Keep up the good work!

When correcting children, keep it positive by using these phrases:

Good try, next time why don't you try...

Is there another way of looking at that?

You're on the right track, but....

That's a good answer, but what about....

You're right, but is there anything you want to add?

Activities For Building Children's Self-Esteem

Activity 1: Write your children encouraging notes telling them something specific and special about them. Put the notes into their lunch boxes tomorrow morning.

Module 2:
Expectations,
Goal Setting,
Motivation, &
Self-Esteem

Part 4
Building
Self-Esteem

Activities For
Building
Children's
Self-Esteem

Module 2:
Expectations,
Goal Setting,
Motivation, &
Self-Esteem

Part 3
Motivating
Children

Activities For
Building
Children's
Self-Esteem

Activity 2: Make compliment pockets for each family member. They can be made from library book pockets (purchase them at a stationary store) or by sealing a No. 10 envelope and cutting three inches off the top. Decorate the pockets with each family member's name and tape to the refrigerator or wall. Use scraps of paper to write compliments to each other and leave them in the pockets. Compliments can be written and left once a week, once a day, or whenever somebody feels like it.

Activity 3: Take a brown paper bag and give one to each of your children. Put out some old magazines and have your children make "Me" bags. Have them decorate the bag by cutting out pictures from the magazines of things they like and gluing them onto the bag. Have them keep the bag and fill it with mementos of the great things they do throughout the year and notes of encouragement from you.

Activity 4: Give everyone in the family a piece of paper and have them draw a picture of themselves on the paper. Pass the papers around allowing each person to write something they like about that person.

You have successfully completed Kids First!™ Module 2. You may now review this module or continue to module 3.

Module 2: Expectations, Goal Setting, Motivation, & Self-Esteem

**Module 3:
Homework**

Homework is an important part of school. Research show that student achievement rises significantly when teachers regularly assign homework and students conscientiously do it.

One research study shows that when low-ability students do just one to three hours of homework a week, their grades are usually as high as those of average-ability students who do not do homework. Similarly, when average-ability students do three to five hours of homework a week, their grades usually equal those of high-ability students who do no homework.

Module 3:
Homework

Module 3:
Homework

In this module you will learn:

● **Why homework is important**
● **How to implement a homework plan**
● **Solutions to the most common homework roadblocks**

43

Why Do Homework?
Homework Serves Several
Important Purposes. It Can:

1. Reinforce classroom learning and extends student's learning beyond the classroom.
2. Teach students to be independent learners.
3. Give students experience in following direction.
4. Give students practice in making judgments and comparisons.
5. Help to develop responsibility and self-discipline.
6. Provide a link between parent and children.

How Much Homework To Expect:

- 1st - 2nd grades: It is recommended that homework may be given from one to three times per week. Usually for 15-30 minutes per night. There are usually no weekend assignments.
- 3rd-4th grades: It is recommended that homework be given two to four times per week. Usually 15-45 minutes per night. There may be occasional weekend assignments and special projects.
- 5th-6th grades: It is recommended that homework assignments be given from two to four times

Module 3:
Homework

Part 1
4-Step
Homework
Plan

Step 2: Do not do the homework for the child. Children need to learn to be independent. Answer questions, help with directions, but let the child do the work. Your children will need more help and guidance when they are younger. You may want to be nearby to help them read directions or to check on their progress, but you will want them to do the work themselves and learn to work independently.

Activity: Sit with your children at the beginning of their homework time. Go through the homework for that day. Ask if there are any questions. Answer the questions and, if necessary, help your children with a problem or two. Then tell your children that you are leaving them to work alone and that they must complete their homework on their own. You may want to set a timer to show how many minutes they need to do their work or show them on a clock

47

Module 3:
Homework

Part 1
4-Step
Homework
Plan

when their homework time is finished. Instruct them that if they finish early they are to read a book for the remainder of the time.

Step 3: Motivate and encourage your children with praise and by showing an interest in their homework.

Activity: At the beginning of your children's study time ask to see their homework. Ask how it relates to what they are studying in class. Look through their homework when they are through and praise them on the effort that went into completing it.

Step 4: Help your children get organized. Buy a special "Homework Folder" for them to keep assignments. Older children will benefit from a planner that allows them to list the assignments they have each day. If you can't find one that is suitable reproduce the form at the end of this module and staple it to a folder. They can follow-up by checking off the assignments completed.

Activity: Go to the store with your children and buy special "Homework" folders. Let your children each pick their own folder. Have them decorate and write _____'s **Homework Folder.** Use this as a safe place to store homework everyday.

Part 2
How to Overcome the 4 Most Common Roadblocks To Homework Success

If your children are having trouble with homework do not hesitate to contact the teacher. He or she will be able to help you with the problems you may be having. He or she will also most likely serve as a valuable partner in helping your children overcome obstacles to successfully completing homework assignments. Below are some of the most common problems and solutions to homework trouble areas.

Problem: Your child forgets her homework at school or forgets the assignment.

Solution:

1. Require that your child get a homework buddy and exchange phone numbers with that buddy. In the event that an assignment is forgotten the child can call the homework buddy and get the assignment from her.
2. If possible, send the child back to school to get the assignment. If the the assignment is not found, tell the child that the next day she is required to

49

Module 3:
Homework

Part 2
How To
Overcome
The 4 Most
Common
Roadblocks
To Homework
Success

make up the work, and this evening she will read or study another subject during homework time.

3. If this is an ongoing problem, make a contract with the child. For   each time she remembers to bring her homework home a star is given. When ten stars are received a reward is earned.

Problem: Your child procrastinates.

Solution:

1. Make it clear that she is expected to do her homework during her study time and that she will not be allowed to leave the study area until she is finished.

2. Use the divide and conquer technique. Break projects down into smaller, more manageable activities. Set a timer for ten minutes and tell her that you will be back to check on her progress. If she has completed her work in that time period then praise or reward her.

3. Set a timer near your child. Turn it on for a specific amount of time. Tell her that she must work for that amount of time. When you return, praise her for what she has accomplished.

4. Plan something rewarding for your child after her homework time i.e., hot chocolate, TV time, play time, etc. This will help motivate her to finish her homework.

Problem: Your child takes forever to complete assignments.

Solution:
1. Set a deadline for the completion of homework. Use a timer or a clock to show when homework time is over.
2. Make sure that there are no distractions where your child is doing homework.
3. Give your child praise or a reward for completing homework on time.
4. Place a piece of graph paper in front of your child. Color a square in for each task that is completed. Give a treat when a pre-set amount of squares are colored (10 for instance).

Problem: Your child will not complete homework on her own.

Solution:
1. Tell your child that you expect her to complete homework assignments on her own and spend five minutes helping her get started. After that, she is expected to complete it by herself.
2. If your child persists in asking for help then give her a piece of paper and tell her each time she asks for help you are going to put a check on the

Module 3:
Homework

Part 2
How To
Overcome
The 4 Most
Common
Roadblocks
To Homework
Success

paper. If she gets less than three checks then she gets a reward.

For more information on homework call this toll free hotline.

Homework Hotline: The National Committee for Citizens in Education is an advocate for citizens who want to improve their children's education. You can call this toll-free helpline if you have questions about homework or other educational issues. 1-800-NETWORK (638-9675)

 You have successfully completed Kids First!™ Module 3. You may now review this module or continue to module 4.

Kids First!

Monday:

Subject	Assignment	Due	Completed

Tuesday:

Subject	Assignment	Due	Completed

Wednesday:

Subject	Assignment	Due	Completed

Thursday:

Subject	Assignment	Due	Completed

Friday:

Subject	Assignment	Due	Completed

**Module 3:
Homework**

**Part 2
How To
Overcome
The 4 Most
Common
Roadblocks
To Homework
Success**

**Homework
Schedule**

Module 4:
Study Skills

Children's IQ's and intelligence have very little to do with how well they do in school. It's really not a matter of how smart children are but how smart they study.

Learning study skills will help your children improve their grades. Students with average ability that do poorly in school do so only because nobody has taught them valuable study skills.

Unfortunately, many schools don't have the time to teach these skills. It is therefore, important for parents to be educated in these techniques and pass them on to their children.

Module 4:
Study Skills

It's not the IQ but the Can Do!

In this module you will learn how to help your children:

- **Read to remember**
- **Take notes**
- **Improve their memories**
- **Study for tests**

Module 4:
Study Skills

Module 4:
Study Skills

Part 1
Reading To
Remember

SQ3R
and
KWL

Part 1
Reading to Remember

Students will remember more of what they read if they use a technique called **SQ3R**. Follow these easy steps:

1. **Skim** - Skim through the material. Read the subheadings. Get a feel for what the main points of the chapter are going to be. Look at the pictures and graphics.

2. **Question** - Ask questions about the chapter. Turn each subheading into a question.

3. **Read** - As you read, answer the questions from the previous step and look for the main ideas.

4. **Recite**- Sit quietly and recall what you just read. Recall the main ideas, important facts, and ideas.

5. **Review** - Look over the material again and check your memory. Review again in a day.

Another technique that helps in retaining more of what is read is called **KWL**. **KWL** stands for what we know (K), what we want to know (W), and what we learned (L).

1. Separate a piece of paper into 3 sections and write

KWL at the top. Put one letter in each section
2. Under the K section write what you know about the topic to be studied.
3. Under the W section write what you want to know about the topic.
4. As you read, write in the L section what you have learned.
5. When finished add any other new information or ideas to the L section.

Activity: Sit down with your children and have them choose a short non-fiction book they enjoy (this will make learning the process more enjoyable and easier to use later). Have them skim, ask questions, read the material, recite, and review the main ideas. Do the same at another time with the KWL technique.

Part 2
Note Taking

Taking notes is an important skill that children should learn in early elementary school. For younger children notes can be made using pictures. Note taking can be used in the classroom and also

Module 4:
Study Skills

Part 2
Note Taking

when studying at home. Here are some easy guidelines for students to follow when taking notes:

● **Notes should be clear and easy to read.**

● **Notes should not include every detail but should include main ideas. Teacher's cues can be used to determine whether something is important or not.**

● **Notes should be organized in a systematic way that is comfortable for the student.**

How to Take Notes:

Each person must find her own way to organize and take notes. Two examples are provided here which can be modified and adjusted to an individual's preference.

1. Get your paper ready for taking notes by drawing a line about 1 1/2 from the margin down one side.

2. Organize the material by giving each main idea a number followed by related facts listed by letters.
3. In the margin draw pictures, time lines, connections with other material, questions, ideas, anything that stands out and that can help clarify or make the material more meaningful later.
4. Use symbols, colored pens or highlighters, or underlining to highlight important concepts.

Module 4:
Study Skills

Part 2
Note Taking

1. Main Idea
  a. Fact
  b. Fact
  c. Fact
2. Next Main Idea
  a. Fact
  b. Fact
  c. Fact
	Pictures
	Symbols
	Time Lines

Another way to take notes is called mapping. Mapping is a relatively new technique derived from research into how the brain assimilates and remembers information.

Mapping Made Easy:

1. Place the main topic to be studied in the center of a page.
2. Add branches (lines) extending from the main idea to important subtopics. Each branch should lead to only one subtopic.
3. Smaller branches are drawn from the subtopic and details added.
4. Student's add personal details to the map to help them remember important information i.e., pictures, symbols, catchy phrases. Adding various colors to the map can make the topic more memorable.

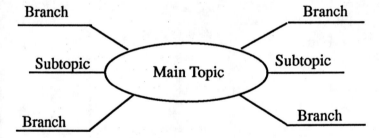

Activity: Have your children choose a book that they enjoy. Go over the different note taking styles. Have your children choose the one that they prefer. Guide your children through taking notes on their chosen book.

Sidebar:

Module 4:
Study Skills

Part 2
How To
Take Notes

Mapping
Made Easy

Part 3
Listening Skills

Listening is an important skill in the classroom. These tips will help children be better listeners.

1. If possible, sit close to the front of the class.
2. Keep your eyes on the teacher.
3. Listen for key terms and main ideas.
4. If you start drifting and thinking about something else, quickly focus back on the teacher.
5. Ask questions and participate in discussions.

Cues To Listen For From The Teacher When Taking Notes:

1. Definitions and key words the teacher gives.
2. List of items the teacher writes on the board.
3. Drawings, charts, overheads or maps the teacher gives the class or emphasizes.
4. Review questions given or posed by the teacher.
5. Key phrases to listen for:
   - "This is important."
   - "This will be on the test."
   - "Be sure to read _____"
   - "Pay attention to _____"

Activity: Have your children practice active listening by sitting attentively and having good eye contact with you. Give your children five sets of directions (three for younger children). Monitor them to see how many of the directions they followed. Give directions such as: put your hands on your head, pick up a pencil, stand up, sit down, count to ten backwards. See how many they can do. Keep practicing until they can listen attentively and do a complete set of directions.

Part 4
Memory

Learning to use one's memory is an important part of studying. Studies show that a person can lose as much as 30 percent of just-learned material in one day if it is not reviewed, and 90 percent in one month!

By teaching your children these important techniques you will be helping them establish studying skills that will last them a lifetime.

1. **Mnemonic Devices -** These are acronyms, rhymes, songs, and patterns. For example, anyone who has studied music has probably used the acronym FACE to learn the notes on the treble.

2. **Chunking** - Grouping small separate bits of information into larger chunks. Our memories can process about seven "chunks" of information at one time. These chunks however are not limited to one item each. For example, lets say your are going to the store and you want to remember to buy the following items: peanut butter, toothpaste, apples, milk, spaghetti sauce, air freshener, and paper towels. To remember you could chunk the food products together and arrange them by spelling a word using the first letter of each item. For instance SPAM= spaghetti sauce, peanut butter, apples, and milk. By grouping the non-food items together, you can form another word: TAP = toothpaste, air freshener, and paper towels. In this way you only have to remember two words instead of 7 items.

3. **Visualizing**- 99.9 percent of people remember things better visually. Therefore, if you can visualize something in your head, it is easier to remember it at a future time. For instance, you have probably heard yourself or someone you know say, "I can remember his face but not his name." To help remember names better, you can associate the name with a visual image. Let's say you meet someone named Jill. You might make the name meaningful by thinking of Jack and Jill. Then associate that thought with a picture in your

Module 4: Study Skills

Part 4 Memory

mind of Jill going up a hill to fetch a pail of water. The more outlandish the visual image is, the more likely you will remember the name.

4. **Note distinguishing characteristics-** The more unique or novel an idea, word, or object is then the more likely we are to remember it. Therefore, when trying to remember something, try to recognize and focus on the properties that make it stand out.

5. **Making something real and meaningful-** The more meaningful and real something is to our own experience, the more likely we are to remember it. In remembering something, it helps to relate it to what we already know.

6. **The place method-** The ancient Greeks used this method to remember speeches. The place method involves selecting a familiar setting such as the rooms in a house. Then, using mental images, associate each room with a name or other information you want to remember.

7. **Repetition-** We remember things that we repeat and rehearse. Reviewing and repeating things will keep them alive in our memories.

8. **Emotions-** People tend to remember things when they are associated with emotional feelings. For instance, most people remember what they were doing when the Space Shuttle Challenger blew up because of the emotional impact it had on them.

Another example is hearing a song that brings back a flood of memories. Therefore, if you want to remember something, associate it with a feeling.

9. **Movement and experience** - People tend to remember things that they have actively been engaged in. Therefore, any movement or activity will increase the retention of materials.

Activity: Go over the above techniques with your children. You may choose to take a few days so as not to overwhelm them. Then, put ten household items into a bag. First, take five out and give your children a minute to memorize them. Ask you children what technique they are going to use. If they do it successfully, increase the number of items to eight. If they have trouble increase the number to six. Keep going and see if they can memorize all ten. You may want to continue this game weekly by changing the items in the bag.

Part 5
Music and Studying

Research shows that listening to classical music can help students concentrate better.

A technique called super-learning was developed by a Bulgarian psychiatrist named Georgi Lozanov. It involves the use of music and other techniques to create a stress free learning environment that is not only enjoyable but also increases motivation in students.

Lozanov discovered that certain forms of Baroque and classical music, especially those with a slow and steady tempo, tend to be physically relaxing and mentally stimulating. Lozanov found that students were able to assimilate and remember material more quickly when the music was playing.

To use super-learning techniques at home, choose classical or Baroque music to play in the background while your children study. Composers to choose form include Haydn, Vivaldi, Pachelbel, Beethoven, and Mozart.

More specifically, Hal A. Lingerman's book *The Healing Energies of Music* suggests playing the following music during studying time:

Bach, Brandenburg Concertos

Telleman, Concerto for Three Violins and
    Orchestra

Brahms, Violin Concerto

Handel, Water Music

> *"I'm not afraid of storms...*
> *for I'm learning how to sail my ship."*
> Louisa May Alcott

Part 6:
Test Taking Skills

Overcoming Test Anxiety.
How You Can Help Your Child:

1. Provide a quiet study area and have your child study over a period of a couple of days. Repeated reviewing will help retain information.
2. Ensure a good night's sleep the day before a test and provide a good breakfast low in sugar.
3. Don't put too much emphasis on test scores. This will cause anxiety in your children. Encourage and praise your children for things they do well. Fear of failure will cause undo anxiety in children.
4. Put an encouraging note in your children's backpack the day of the test and say a word or two of encouragement as they leave for school.
5. Review test results with your child. Discuss wrong answers and find out why she answered that way. Often times a child will misunderstand a question and discussing it can help the child not make the same mistakes in the future.

Module 4:
Study Skills

Part 6
Test Taking
Skills

Overcoming
Test Anxiety

Module 4:
Study Skills

Part 6
Test Taking
Skills

Test Taking
Strategies

Preparing For The Test:
A 3 Day Plan to Higher Test Scores

● **Day 1-** Take notes and review text and/or materials.

● **Day 2-** Use the memorization techniques in Part 4 of this module to make acronyms of key words and concepts, make visual representations, act things out, use repetition, etc., until you are familiar with the material.

● **Day 3-** Make and take a practice test. This can be done on a piece of paper or by having someone ask you questions about the material.

Test Taking Strategies:

1. Read the directions carefully and ask the teacher questions on any directions you don't understand. Many students miss a question because they fail to read the directions <u>carefully</u> or only read the first part of a question.

2. If you don't know the answer to a question put a mark next to it and come back at the end. Don't dwell or get frustrated over any one answer. If after coming back to it, the answer is still not apparent then guess.

3. If the correct answer is not immediately obvious,

use the process of elimination to narrow down your choices.

4. On true/false questions words such as never, always, and all are clues that the answer stands a greater chance of being false. Whereas, questions with words like most, normally, and sometimes are most likely to be true.

5. If any part of a true/false question is false then the entire item is false.

6. On matching tests, first match the answers you know for sure.

7. On essay tests be sure that you read the questions carefully. Then, organize your answer to include all parts of the question. Be succinct and use many facts to support your answers. Write as neatly as possible. Studies show that higher grades are given to papers that look neater.

8. At the end of a test allow five minutes to go over answers. Check that <u>all</u> question were read completely and answered correctly.

Activity 1: Have your child make a practice test for an upcoming test. Have your child make essay questions, true/false, matching, and multiple choice questions. Go through each of the above steps and practice taking the test.

Module 4:
Study Skills

Part 6
Test Taking
Skills

Test Taking
Strategies

69

Module 4:
Study Skills

Part 6
Test Taking
Skills

Test Taking
Strategies

Activity 2: Take an old test your child has completed and go through it together. Read the directions and look at the types of question on the test. Talk about the mistakes and how they could have been avoided. Use the test as a learning tool for future tests.

You have successfully completed Kids First!™ Module 4. You may now review this module and continue to module 5.

Module 4:
Study Skills

> *Take time for all things...*
> *great haste make waste.*
> Benjamin Franklin

71

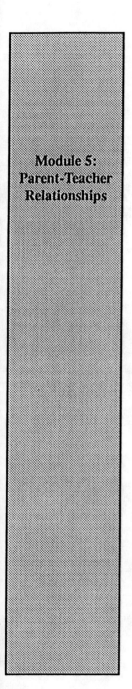

**Module 5:
Parent-Teacher
Relationships**

Module 5:
Parent-Teacher Relationships

In this module you will learn:

- How to make the most of parent-teacher relationships
- What to ask at parent conferences
- How to approach a teacher when your children are having problems
- How to become involved in your children's school
- What to do if you suspect your child has a learning disability

Part 1
5 Ways To Build A Positive Relationship With Your Children's Teacher:

1. Stop in during the first week of school to introduce yourself. After the initial contact keep open the lines of communication. Don't assume things are going well with your children's education if you don't hear anything from the teacher.
2. Attend Back-To-School Night and parent conferences.
3. Volunteer in the classroom if you can. Working parents can help by taking a day off work to attend a field trip or other special activity. The teacher can send things home for you to do.
4. Join the school's PTA or PTO.
5. If there's a problem your children are having at school, contact the teacher and discuss possible solutions. Remember, the teacher can be a valuable partner in helping overcome difficulties.

Module 5:
Parent-Teacher
Relationships

Part 2
What Parents
Should Know
At The
Beginning
Of The Year
Regarding
Their Child's
Classroom

Part 2
What Parents Should Know
At The Beginning Of The Year
Regarding Their Child's Classroom

Most of these items should be covered at Back-To-School Night. Take these questions with you and write down the answers. Check with the teacher for those questions not covered.

75

Module 5:
Parent-Teacher
Relationships

Part 2
What Parents
Should Know
At The
Beginning
Of The Year
Regarding
Their Child's
Classroom

1. What time does school begin and end?
2. What time are students allowed to arrive at school?
3. What supplies does my child need for school?
4. What time are my child's breaks? Is there a snack break before lunch?
5. When may my child use the restrooms?
6. What time is lunch? What if my child wants to buy lunch?
7. What is the classroom discipline plan? What are the classroom rules?
8. What are the consequences for not following those rules? What are the positive incentives for following the rules?
9. What is the classroom homework policy? How much time should be set aside for homework each night?
10. What subjects will be covered this year?
11. What is the policy on late and make-up work?
12. When are spelling tests given? How many words per week?
13. Is there a library time? If so, when are books due each week?
14. Is there a system for communicating with the teacher on a weekly, bi-monthly, or monthly basis?
15. Is there a way to check on my child's progress other than report cards and parent conferences?

Part 3
Parent -Teacher Conferences

Do's and Don'ts Of Parent Conferences:

● Do plan ahead. Write down observations, questions, etc., that you want to discuss.
● Do talk to your child before the conference. Find out if there anything she would like discussed or that she is concerned about.
● Do work positively with the teacher on areas of concern. Come up with a plan and follow through on your part of the plan.
● Do share with the teacher any information that might help her understand your child better i.e., a recent divorce, a move to a new neighborhood, a death in the family, etc.
● Don't become angry or defensive. The teacher is only trying to help.
● Don't be intimidated by the teacher.

These questions can be taken to the parent-teacher conferences and used as a reference for discussion points.

1. What are my child's areas of strength?
2. What are my child's areas of weakness?
3. Describe my child's work habits. Does she finish

Module 5:
Parent-Teacher
Relationships

Part 3
Parent-Teacher
Conferences

Do's And Don'ts
Of Parent
Conferences

Module 5:
Parent-Teacher
Relationships

Part 3
Parent-Teacher
Conferences

Action Plan:
Ways The
Teacher & I
Can Work
Together
To Help
My Child

assignments on time? Does she give her best effort?

4. How does my child behave socially? Does she get along with others? Is she shy? Is she too aggressive? Does she have friends?

5. How is my child's behavior in class? Does she respect the teacher and follow the class rules?

6. How are my child's listening skills? Does she follow directions?

7. How is my child's homework? Is it being turned in completed and on time?

If action is required, use the following plan to determine ways you and the teacher can work together to help your child.

Action Plan:
Ways The Teacher And I Can Work Together To Help My Child:

A. What the teacher will do:

_____

_____

B. What I will do:

_____

_____

78

C. What my child will do:

_____

_____

D. Follow-up (How we will check the progress: phone calls, weekly progress report, notes, etc.)

_____

_____

Part 4
What to do If You Suspect Your Child has a Learning Disability

Part 4
What To Do
If You
Suspect Your
Child Has A
Learning
Disability

Nearly 4 million school-age children have learning disabilities, yet not all learning problems are necessarily learning disabilities. Many children are simply slower developmentally at learning certain skills. What seems to be a learning disability may simply be a delay in maturation. Some common types of learning disabilities are:

● Developmental and speech language disorders— children with speech and language disorders have difficulty producing speech sounds, using spoken language to communicate, or understanding what other people say.

● Academic skills disorders—students with this dis-

79

Module 5:
Parent-Teacher
Relationships

Part 4
What To Do
If You
Suspect Your
Child Has A
Learning
Disability

order are often years behind their classmates in developing reading, writing, or arithmetic skills.

● Attention disorders—this leaves students unable to focus their attention. Sometimes these students appear to daydream excessively, and once their attention is attained they are easily distracted. In a large proportion of affected children—mostly boys—the attention deficit is accompanied by hyperactivity. This is called attention deficit hyperactivity disorder (ADHD).

If you think your child may have a learning disability or the teacher has suggested this may be the case, the following will probably happen:

1. Most likely, the teacher and the parent will meet and discuss the concerns about the child. A plan may be put into place with modifications in the classroom and at home to help the child. Modifications may be changing the child's seat, reducing classwork and homework, giving the child manipulatives to use in class, etc.

2. After about six weeks, the modifications are reviewed. If improvement is seen, then most likely the modifications are working and the student's progress will continue to be monitored. If, however, the student is not improving, the student will probably be referred to the school psychologist

and special education teacher for testing.

3. By law, learning disabilities is defined as a significant gap between a person's intelligence and the skills that the person has achieved at each age.

     If the tests indicate a learning disability then an Individualized Educational Plan (IEP) is developed. The plan outlines the specific skills that the child needs to develop. The specialist will also recommend the type of assistance thta the child will receive. This will depend on the learning disability.
     In most ways, children with learning disabilities are no different from children without these disabilities. At school, they eat together and share sports, games, and after-school activities. But since they have specific learning needs, most schools provide special programs.
     Schools typically provide special education programs either in a separate all-day classroom or as a special education class that the student attends for several hours each week. If the problems are severe, some parents may choose to place their child in a special school for the learning disabled.

Parent Rights

● The Individuals with Disabilities Education Act of 1990 assures a public education to school-aged

Module 5:
Parent-Teacher
Relationships

Part 4
What To Do
If You
Suspect Your
Child Has A
Learning
Disability

Parent
Rights

children with diagnosed learning disabilities.

● Parents have the right to appeal the school's decision if they disagree with the findings of the diagnostic team.

● Parents also have the right to request an outside evaluation. The school district's policies will determine who pays for this.

● Publicly funded colleges and universities must also remove barriers that keep out disabled students. As a result, many colleges now recruit and work with students with learning disabilities to make it possible for them to attend.

For more information on learning disabilities contact the following organizations:

Council for Exceptional Children (both handicapped and gifted)
4156 Association Drive
Reston, VA 22091

Association for Children and Adults with Learning Disabilities
4156 Library Road
Pittsburgh, PA 15234

Kids First!

For information on ADD or ADHD contact:

Children with Attention Deficit Disorders
1859 Birth Pine Island Road
Suite 185
Plantation, FL 33322

Module 5:
Parent-Teacher
Relationships

Part 5
Gifted &
Talented
Education

Part 5
Gifted and Talented Education

● The Gifted and Talented Act has defined gifted and talented as those students having an outstanding ability to achieve intellectually, creatively, in visual or performing arts or in leadership.

● Most schools use IQ and achievement tests to determine which students are gifted. While a student may get top grades, it does not necessarily mean that she is "gifted." Often times parents will put undo pressure on their children by deciding they are gifted when they are not.

● Gifted students usually do things earlier, better, and differently than other students. These students usually have unusually high abilities in reading, math, music, or creativity at an early age.

● If your child is indeed gifted. Learn what programs are available at your school and what training the teachers of these programs are given. Find

83

out what the school's philosophy is about gifted education and whether there are magnet schools that your child can attend.

● Discuss with the teacher ways that the student will be challenged in class and what you can do at home to challenge your child.

These National Associations can provide information for parents:

Council for Exceptional Children (both handicapped and gifted)
4156 Association Drive
Reston, VA 22091

Association for the Gifted (TAG)
(a division of the council for Exceptional Children)
C/O James Alvino
P.O. Box 115
Sewell, NJ 08080

National Association for Gifted Children (NAGC)
4175 Lovell Road
Circle Pines, MN 55014

Program for the Education of the Gifted and Talented
U.S. Department of Government
400 Maryland Avenue, S.W.
Washington, D.C. 20202

Module 5:
Parent-Teacher
Relationships

Part 5
Gifted &
Talented
Education

Organizations

You have successfully completed Kids First!™ Module 5. You may now review this module or continue to module 6.

**Module 5:
Parent-Teacher
Relationships**

**Module 6:
Teaching
Your Children
Discipline &
Responsibility**

Module 6
Teaching Your Children
Discipline and Responsibility

In this module you will learn:

- **How to implement an easy to use discipline plan**
- **Valuable ways to teach your children responsibility**
- **Ways to teach your children values**

Part 1
Discipline

Module 6:
Teaching
Your Children
Discipline &
Responsibility

Part 1
Discipline

Children need discipline and consistency in their lives. Teachers report that many students are starting school with very little self-discipline. Self-discipline influences children's behavior in the classroom, and is one of the basic requirements for achievement. Studies have found that children from homes with clear structure, shared responsibilities, and set routines learned better in school than children from homes with no consistent rules.

Even though kids will constantly test and push the limits of parents, parents need to have a discipline policy that is consistently and fairly enforced.

Many parents think of discipline as punishing, yelling, or nagging at children. A good discipline program, however, should be based on positive ways to help children learn self-control, acceptable behavior, and making wise choices on their own.

Research shows that physical punishment like slapping or spanking, or verbal abuse like yelling and shouting are ineffective discipline methods. In the long run, these methods are often more harmful than useful in that they demoralize children and do not help develop self-control.

Kids First!

Activity: Discipline need not be a burden. Discipline can be a positive experience in your home by following this helpful plan. To begin, use this area to write and reflect upon the discipline plan you currently have in your household.

What are the rules in your household?

_____

How are those rules enforced?

_____

What are the consequences for not following the rules?

_____

What are the rewards for following the rules?

_____

Does your child follow the rules?

_____

Do you consistently follow through on enforcing the rules? If not, give an example of when you might give in on a rule.

_____

What frustrations do you face in enforcing rules in your home?

_____

**Module 6:
Teaching
Your Children
Discipline &
Responsibility**

**Part 1
Discipline**

Don't feel alone if when reflecting on the above questions you discovered some frustrations in enforcing rules in your home. Many parents either don't have a discipline plan at home or abandon one in the face of resistance. If that is the case in your home then the following plan can be easily implemented.

Activity: Family Discipline Plan

Follow these step-by-step instructions to implementing a positive family-oriented discipline plan in your household:

1. Sit down as a family and establish a minimum of three and a maximum of five clear and concise rules for you home. Children are less likely to break rules that they have helped make. Write the rules on a piece of paper or posterboard. Children who are old enough can write the rules for you while the younger ones decorate the rule sign. Post the rules in a conspicuous place in your home (like the refrigerator). The rules may look like this:

---

1) Homework must be completed every day.
2) Chores must be done everyday.
3) There will be no talking back to parents.

Module 6:
Teaching
Your Children
Discipline &
Responsibility

Part 1
Discipline

Family
Discipline
Plan

2. Discuss the rules with your children and give examples of following the rules. Then ask them if they have any questions about the rules.

3. Establish consequences for the rules. Consequences should be simple, non-physical, and something that you can easily follow through with. Time-outs are an effective consequence. Other examples include:

● There will be no TV watching until homework is complete.

● There will be no playing until chores are completed.

● If you talk back to your parents you will spend 15 minutes in your room with no TV or activities.

4. Establish rewards for following the rules. You may want to make a sticker chart and give a sticker each day a rule is followed. You can also determine rewards on a weekly basis, i.e., going out for pizza if all homework is completed that week.

● Rewards should be brainstormed together and meaningful to the child. Some favorites are: an ice cream cone, going out for pizza, having a friend spend the night, or staying up late one weekend night.

● Another way to give rewards is buy a couple of trinkets or candies and put them into a grab bag. When the child reaches her goal, she can reach into the grab bag for her reward.

Module 6:
Teaching
Your Children
Discipline &
Responsibility

Part 1
Discipline

Family
Discipline
Plan

Module 6:
Teaching
Your Children
Discipline &
Responsibility

Part 1
Discipline

Enforcing
The Rules

● An often overlooked reward is praise. Praise should be given on a daily basis to children who follow the rules. For example;

—"I really like how you finished your homework on time tonight."

—"I really liked how you didn't talk back to me when I asked you to clean up your room today."

—"I really like how you did your chores today without being asked."

Enforcing The Rules:

1. Consistency. Consistency. Consistency. Consistency is the key to any discipline system. Kids will push and try to bend the rules. It is your job to consistently follow through on the rules. If you have a partner, it is important that you enforce the house rules together. Children will become adept at playing one parent off the other. Always present a united front.

2. If a child argues with you simply restate the rule and the consequence for not following the rule. This is called the broken record technique because you repeat the same message again and again.

Parent: "I'm sorry, but you did not finish your homework, there will be no TV watching tonight."

Child: "But I will finish it now."

Parent: "I'm sorry but you did not finish it by the

time we agreed upon. There will be no TV watching tonight."

Child: "I'm sorry, I won't do it again. I promise."

Parent: "I'm sorry too, but you did not finish your homework, there will be no TV watching tonight."

What To Do If Your Child Throws A Tantrum:

1. Stay calm. Try not to get angry and caught up in the drama of the moment. Take a deep breath and count to five. Detach yourself from the situation.
2. Calmly and firmly tell the child that under no circumstance is this behavior acceptable. Do not try to reason with a child in this condition. Tell the child you will talk to her later when she can behave appropriately.
3. Remove the child to her room for a time-out period. Tell her that she will receive a consequence of _____. Be sure to follow through later on the consequence if the child does not obey.
4. Leave the child in her room.
5. If the child does not remain in her room then repeat steps 1-4.

Module 6:
Teaching
Your Children
Discipline &
Responsibility

Part 1
Discipline

What To Do
If Your Child
Throws
A Tantrum

Part 2
Teaching Responsibility

> *Responsibility is the price of greatness.*
> Winston Churchill

Children need to be taught to be responsible for themselves and for others. Studies show that many children see nothing wrong with cheating on tests. Others see nothing wrong with taking things that don't belong to them. Studies show that belief in the work ethic and taking responsibility for one's actions are important predictors for student success. Teaching children at a young age that hard work and effort lead to success will encourage children to develop habits that will follow them to adulthood.

Remember, parents are their children's first teachers. Therefore, what we say, and more importantly, what we *do* will be what our children learn.

Responsible Behavior Consists Of The Following:

● **Practicing Honesty**
● **Showing respect and compassion for others**
● **Showing courage in standing up for our principles**

- **Developing self-control in acting on our principles**
- **Maintaining self-respect**

Honesty - Honesty means telling the truth. You can model honest to your child by telling her the truth. You can also show your children how sometimes being honest means facing up to your own mistakes and learning from those mistakes.

Respect and Compassion for others - Children need to show respect and concern for the well-being of others. Children should learn empathy (Putting themselves in the shoes of another and seeing things from another's point of view). Children should be taught to treat people fairly regardless of race, sex, or ethnic group. Children should also be taught the golden rule: Do unto others as we would have others do unto us.

Courage- Courage is the ability to stand up for what one believes and doing what one believes is right even in the face of adversity. Courage does not mean not being afraid. It takes courage to be afraid and still overcome a fear like being afraid of the dark. Children need to know that sometimes it is all right to be afraid. An example is if a younger child sees an older child trying to steal a bike. The older child

Module 6: Teaching Your Children Discipline & Responsibility

Part 2 Responsibility

Responsible Behavior Consists Of:

95

Module 6:
Teaching
Your Children
Discipline &
Responsibility

Part 2
Responsibility

How Parents
Can Encourage
Responsible
Behavior

says, "If you tell, I'm going to beat you up after school." The child may be afraid of the consequence, but the right thing to do is to tell on the child.

Self-control- Self control is the ability to resist acting inappropriately in order to act responsibly. It involves persistence and patience and the ability to give up immediate gratification for long term rewards.

Self-Respect- People with self-respect believe in themselves. They know that they may fail but still make an effort to achieve. They try their hardest and learn from their mistakes.

How Parents Can Encourage Responsible Behavior:

1. Use everyday experiences to teach responsibility. We can show by our words and action how to treat ourselves and others with respect. For instance, let's say you find a wallet as you and your children are walking into a grocery store. You have two choices:
● Check it for money and keep it.
● Turn it in to the store manager.
● In instance one, you are modeling the behavior that it's all right to keep something that isn't yours.

In instance two, you are modeling the behavior that when something that isn't yours, you try to return it to its owner. Which one do you want your children to learn?

2. Use literature and stories to teach valuable lessons. When a child loves a story and you point out an important lesson learned from it, she will remember it. *The Book of Virtues* by William Bennett is loaded with valuable learning stories.

3. Talk and encourage your children to learn about different lands and different people. Discuss news stories about different countries. Talk about different customs celebrated during holiday seasons.

4. Teach your children manners. Teach them how to say please and thank you, to write thank you notes, how to eat at the dinner table, to say excuse me when they bump into somebody, not to interrupt people when they are talking, etc.

5. Teach the value of giving to your children. Some parents feel that they must give material things to their children to make them happy. This teaches children that receiving is more important than giving. Take your children to an orphanage, homeless shelter, or other place for the needy and give homemade gifts to people less fortunate than themselves.

6. Teach your children how to assert themselves and how to say "No" to peer pressure. Role play with

Module 6: Teaching Your Children Discipline & Responsibility

Part 2 Responsibility

How Parents Can Encourage Responsible Behavior

Module 6:
Teaching
Your Children
Discipline &
Responsibility

Part 2
Responsibility

How Parents
Can Encourage
Responsible
Behavior

your children so they can practice. Teach your children to use " I" messages when somebody does something that bothers them. They should say the following to the person:

I feel _____

when you _____

because _____

And I want you _____

7. Make sure your children have specific chores and duties they are responsible for around the house.

8. Talk to your children about choosing their friends wisely. Discuss what a friend is and also what one isn't.

Activity: Complete the following questions on the ways you can model and teach your children responsible behavior.

Three ways I can model and teach my children honesty.

1_____

2._____

3._____

Kids First!

Three ways I can model or teach empathy to my children.
1._____

2._____

3._____

Three ways I can model or teach courage to my children.
1._____

2._____

3._____

Three ways I can model or teach self-control to my children.
1._____

2._____

3._____

Module 6:
Teaching
Your Children
Discipline &
Responsibility

Part 2
Responsibility

How Parents
Can Encourage
Responsible
Behavior

Module 6:
Teaching
Your Children
Discipline &
Responsibility

Part 2
Responsibility

How Parents
Can Encourage
Responsible
Behavior

Three ways I can model or teach self-respect to my children.

1._____

2._____

3._____

You have successfully completed Kids First!™ Module 6. You may now review this module or continue to module 7.

Kids First!

Module 6:
Teaching
Your Children
Discipline &
Responsibility

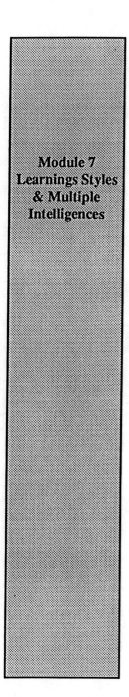

**Module 7
Learnings Styles
& Multiple
Intelligences**

Module 7
Learning Styles and
Multiple Intelligences

In this module you will learn:

● **The three most common learning styles**
● **How to determine what learning style your child prefers**
● **About the seven intelligences**
● **Your children's intelligence strengths and weaknesses**
● **How to apply this information in helping your children learn and study better**

Module 7
Learnings Styles
& Multiple
Intelligences

Part 1
Learning Styles

Module 7
Learnings Styles
& Multiple
Intelligences

Part 1
Learning Styles

There are three learning styles. Children draw on all three when learning, but most children have one style that is more dominate. Recognizing your children's preferred learning styles will help you to focus them on strategies that utilize that particular style.

1. Visual - These children learn best by seeing. They should focus on visual cues from the teacher and use mapping and visualizing when studying.

2. Auditory - These children learn best by hearing. They usually like music and listening activities. Learning strategies for them include the use of music, songs, tape recorders, and verbal directions.

3. Kinesthetic - These student learn by moving. They learn best by doing and using hands-on manipulatives. Learning and studying strategies should include moving around, using the body, and using physical materials that can be manipulated.

Assessing the learning style of your children is as easy as observing them at home or talking to their teachers at school. Does your child like looking at pictures? Does your child enjoy listening to music, books on tape, stories? Does your child move around a lot?

Ask your children's teaches if they can follow oral directions? Or do they need visual cues? Is your child in trouble a lot for not sitting still? Does your child have trouble keeping her hands to herself? These observations can usually tell you what style your child prefers.

Part 2
Multiple Intelligences

Many parents want to know how intelligent their children are. First, however, parents need to realize that the current view of intelligence is changing. Recent research in education has shown that there is not one, but seven identified intelligences.

Since the early 1900's when Albert Binet pioneered the development of the IQ test, it has been assumed there is only one intelligence. Questioning the belief in a unitary intelligence, Harvard University Education Professor Howard Gardner has developed his own explanation of intelligence.

Gardner's research led him to see that a wider

Module 7
Learnings Styles
& Multiple
Intelligences

Part 2
Multiple
Intelligences

Module 7
Learnings Styles
& Multiple
Intelligences

Part 2
Multiple
Intelligences

variety of intelligences exist and thus to his theory of multiple intelligences. In his book, *Frames of Mind: The Theory of Multiple Intelligences*, Gardner proposes that children draw on seven different sets of core abilities or intelligences to process various kinds of information, solve problems, or produce products valued by society. Each child possesses all seven intelligences, but children tend to be stronger in two or three. These are important to know because they can affect the way in which you child learns and studies best.

The characteristics of each intelligence are:

1. **Linguistic** (word smart) -They like reading, writing, telling stories and jokes, and playing word games. This is the intelligence of authors, journalists, and lawyers.
2. **Logical/Mathematical** (math smart) -They enjoy math, working on computers and with calculators. They like doing experiments and solving problems, exploring patterns, and working with numbers and logic. Einstein tapped into this intelligence when he developed his theory of relativity.
3. **Spatial** (picture smart) - This is characterized by an ability to think in pictures. These people enjoy reading maps or charts, drawing, painting, or other art activities. Individuals like Pablo Picasso,

and Ansel Adams were strong in this intelligence.

4. **Musical** (music smart)- These people like to hum, sing, tap rhythms, play an instrument, and are sensitive to sounds in the environment. This is the intelligence of Bach, Brahms, and Mozart.

5. **Bodily-Kinesthetic** (body smart)- They like to move around, touch, act, dance, make crafts, and participate in sports. Athletes, mechanics, and surgeons use this intelligence.

6. **Interpersonal** (people smart) - They have many friends and enjoy being with people. They prefer to work in groups and are good at understanding the feelings of others. Ronald Reagan was a master of this intelligence.

7. **Intrapersonal** (self smart)- These people enjoy working alone. They are independent, self-confident, and good at assessing their strengths and weaknesses. Psychologists, entrepreneurs, and self-made people are highly competent in this intelligence.

Module 7
Learnings Styles
& Multiple
Intelligences

Part 2
Multiple
Intelligences

To help children develop an awareness of their intelligences, begin by taking the survey at the end of this module. Afterward, talk to them about intelligence. Explain that there are many ways a student is smart and discuss the seven intelligences.

Remember, the important thing to remember

when discussing intelligence is not how smart is your child, but how is your child smart.

Activities To Do That Promote Or Enhance Each Intelligence:

● **Linguistic** - Read stories, write stories, letters, or in a journal, play word games like scrabble or crossword puzzles, tell stories, choral read, attend story telling/book readings at the local library. Studies and learns best by saying, hearing, and seeing words.

● **Logical/Mathematical** - Do brain teasers, logic and number games, and science experiments with your children. Encourage the use of computers, calculators, mental calculation, and pattern recognition. Visit science museums, subscribe to science magazines, and read about famous scientists, inventors, and mathematicians. Studies and learns best by categorizing, solving problems, and classifying.

● **Spatial** - Provide art classes or art materials in the home, play imagination games, do mind-mapping, read maps together, draw, and do jigsaw puzzles and mazes. Studies and learns best by seeing and visualizing.

● **Bodily-Kinesthetic** - Provide hands-on learning materials. Encourage drama, dance, sports, and handicrafts such as sewing, building models, sculpting, etc. Studies and learns best by touching and manipulating materials.

- **Musical** - Sing with your child. Provide music lessons, listen to music together, go to concert, play classical music while he or she is studying. Buy musical tapes that teach educational concepts like adding, multiplication, parts of speech, etc. Studies and learns best through rhythm, melody, and music.

- **Interpersonal** - Provide cooperative learning experiences with the family. Encourage your child to join clubs, participate in group and community activities, peer mediate at school, or run for class officer. Studies and learns best by working in groups or by interacting with people.

- **Intrapersonal** - Encourage your child to write in a journal. Allow time for independent study and the pursuit of personal hobbies or interests. Studies and learns best by working alone and /or thinking and reflecting.

Module 7
Learnings Styles
& Multiple
Intelligences

Part 2
Multiple
Intelligences

Activities
To Do That
Promote Or
Enhance
Each
Intelligence

Multiple Intelligence Survey

Module 7
Learnings Styles
& Multiple
Intelligences

Part 2
Multiple
Intelligences

Multiple
Intelligence
Survey

This survey will give you a general idea of what intelligence preferences your child has. Read it to them if they are too young to read it by themselves and us the following scale to describe your child:

5= strongly agree   4= agree   3= sometimes agree
2= disagree   1= disagree strongly

_____1.   I am good at reading.
_____2.   I like to spend time alone.
_____3.   I spend a lot of time with friends.
_____4.   I am good at making things with my hands.
_____5.   I listen to music a lot.
_____6.   I enjoy having people around.
_____7.   I'm good at reading maps, charts, and diagrams.
_____8.   I like to sit quietly and think.
_____9.   I am good at math.
_____10. I am good at singing.
_____11. I am good at crossword puzzles or word games.
_____12. I am good at sports.
_____13. Adding numbers quickly in my head is easy.
_____14. I am good at drawing and art.

_____15. I am good at computer programming

_____16. I am good at playing a musical instrument.

_____17 I like working in a group better than working alone.

_____19. I am good at writing stories.

_____20. It is easy for me to picture things in my head.

_____21. I am good at solving my own problems alone.

_____22. I move, tap, twitch, or fidget while sitting.

_____23. I like to have music on when I am studying.

_____24. I like moving around, touching, or acting things out.

_____25. I am good at telling jokes and stories.

_____26. I work best when I'm allowed to work alone.

_____27. I am good at jigsaw puzzles or mazes.

_____28. It is easy for me to make new friends.

**Module 7
Learnings Styles
& Multiple
Intelligences**

**Part 2
Multiple
Intelligences**

**Multiple
Intelligence
Survey**

Module 7
Learnings Styles
& Multiple
Intelligences

Part 2
Multiple
Intelligences

Multiple
Intelligence
Survey

Scoring:
Add up the scores for the numbers next to each intelligence and write the total on the line.

Linguistic -	1, 11, 19, 25	Total: _____
Logical/ Mathematical	9, 13, 15, 17	Total: _____
Spatial -	7, 14, 20, 27	Total: _____
Bodily/ Kinesthetic	4, 12, 22, 24	Total: _____
Musical	5, 10, 16, 23	Total: _____
Intrapersonal	2, 8, 21, 26	Total: _____
Interpersonal	3, 6, 18, 28	Total: _____

If your child scored:

16-20: Your child is very comfortable with this intelligence. It probably comes naturally to her.

10-15: Your child is moderately comfortable with this intelligence. Exposure to activities in this intelligence would enhance her comfort level.

0-9: This is an intelligence area that your child probably does not feel very comfortable. Activities that expose your child to this intelligence would help encourage her development in this area.

Kids First!

 You have successfully completed Kids First!™ Module 7. You may now review this module or continue to module 8.

Module 7
Learnings Styles
& Multiple
Intelligences

**Module 8
Reading**

The more you read, the smarter you grow. The smarter you grow the longer you stay in school. The longer you stay in school, the more money you earn. The more you earn, the better your children will do in school. So if you hook a child with reading, you influence not only his future but also that of the next generation.

Jim Trelease
author of *The Read Aloud Handbook*

Module 8
Reading

Module 8
Reading

In this module you will learn:

- **How to instill a love of reading in your children**
- **How to motivate your children to read**
- **How to help your children read better**
- **About recommended books for children to read**

Part 1
Reading Is Fun!

Reading is the single most important skill your child will learn. Unfortunately, studies show that only 22 percent of eighth-graders read daily for fun, while 65 percent watch three hours or more of television everyday.

The Center for the study of Reading and The National Council of Teachers of English confirm that reading builds vocabulary, stimulates imagination, stretches the attention span, nourishes emotional development, and introduces the English language.

Ways To Enhance Reading Success In Your Children:

● Read to your children everyday. Jim Trelease says this is the most important thing you can do for your children. In fact, he feels that reading is the single most important social factor in American life today.

● Listen to your children read. Encourage older children to read to younger brothers and sisters.

● Have a regular D.E.A.R. (Drop Everything and

Read) family time in your home every evening.
- Let your children see you reading for pleasure.
- Take your children to the library every week.
- Keep a large supply of books, magazines, newspapers, and other reading materials in the house.
- Limit your children's TV viewing time.
- Subscribe to your children's favorite magazines.
- Set up a library in your house. Encourage your children to lend and borrow books with friends.
- Use special incentives to encourage reading. Set up a star chart for books read and reward your children when a certain predetermined number of books have been completed. Allow your children to stay up an extra 1/2 hour each evening to read.
- Choose a night each week for family member's to read a book of their choice to the family.

Part 2
Reading Activities

> *Reading is to the mind*
> *what exercise is to the body.*
> Joseph Addison

For young children:
1. Pick a story or poem that repeats phrases. Give your child a phrase to repeat each time you read a new part of the story.

Module 8
Reading

Part 2
Reading
Activities

2. Read a portion of the story or poem, then stop and let your child repeat the phrase.
3. Encourage your child to act out the story.
4. Teach alphabet recognition by making cookies in the shape of alphabet letters. Have your children help mold the cookie dough to look like the letters and decorate them.

Some good books with repetitive patterns are *Alexander and The Terrible, Horrible, No Good, Very Bad Day,* by Judith Viorst; *Brown Bear, Brown Bear, What Do You See?* by Bill Martin, Jr.; *Green Eggs and Ham* by Dr. Seuss; and *The Little Engine that could* by Watty Piper.

For beginning readers:
1. Find a story, poem or tongue twister that repeats sounds and letters.
2. Point out these sounds and letters. Explain that they often make the same sound whenever you see them with other letters on the page. For example:
3. There once was a fAt cAt named Matt. And a blAck cAt who hAd a big bAt. The rAt put a tAck when the cAt turned his bAck on the mAt where the blAck cAt sAt.
4. Make a bingo grid of alphabet letters in mixed order. Give your child some beans, buttons, or

other covering pieces. Play bingo by calling out a sound. When your child gets 5 letters covered in a row give her a prize.

4. Help your child make an alphabet book. Each page has a letter and a picture or word that goes with that letter. Staple the book together and let the whole family read it together.

For more advanced readers:

1. Ask your child to read to you.
2. Take turns reading with your child. Read one paragraph and have your child read the next one. Or take turns reading full pages one after the other. Keep in mind that your child may be concentrating on how to read, and that your reading helps to keep the story alive.
3. Story talk. While reading a story with your child pause and ask questions. What do you think will happen next? Why do you think that happened? When finished discuss the story with your child. Ask what she liked or didn't like about the story. Ask what characters she liked or related to and why.
4. Make puppets by drawing the characters in a story on paper, cutting them out and gluing them to popsicle sticks, or decorating paper bags in the likeness of each character. Your child can then have a puppet show reading and acting out the

parts of the various characters.

5. Have your child relate the story to personal experiences. Ask if anything like that has ever happened to her before.

If Your Child Has Trouble Reading The Words You Can Help By:

Module 8
Reading

Part 2
Reading
Activities

If Your
Child Has
Trouble
Reading The
Words You
Can Help By:

Book Resources

● Having your child skip over the work, read the rest of the sentence, and ask what word would make sense in the story.

● Have your child use what they know about letters and sounds to help sound out the word.

● Supply the word for her and keep on reading: enjoyment is the main goal.

● Praise your child on her effort and skills.

Book Resources

The following organizations publish lists of children's books and are available free or at a nominal cost:

American Library Association
Publications Order Department
50 East Huron Street
Chicago, IL 60611

Kids First!

International Reading Association
800 Barksdale Road
P.O. Box 8139
Newark, DE 19714-8139

Reading is Fundamental, Inc.
Publications Department
Smithsonian Institution
600 Maryland Avenue, SW, Suite 500
Washington, D.C. 20024-2520

The following books contain lists and suggestions of books suitable for children:

Kimmel, Margaret Mary. *For Reading Out Loud: A Guide to Sharing Books with Children*. Delacorte Press.

Larrick, Nancy. *A Parent's Guide to Children's Reading*, 5th edition. Bantam Books.

Russell, William F., ed. *Classics to Read Aloud to Your Children*, 1984 edition. Crown.

Trelease, Jim. *The New Read-Aloud Handbook*. Penguin Handbooks.

 You have successfully completed Kids First!™ Module 8. You may now review this module or continue to module 9.

Module 8
Reading

Part 2
Reading
Activities

Book Resources

**Module 9:
Learning
Is Fun!
Activities
Parents Can
Do To Instill
A Love Of
Learning**

*I hear, and I forget;
I see, and I remember;
I do, and I understand.*
-Chinese Proverb

Module 9
Learning is Fun!
Activities Parents Can Do To Instill A Love Of Learning.

Module 9:
Learning
Is Fun!
Activities
Parents Can
Do To Instill
A Love Of
Learning

In this module you will learn:

● **Fun activities to do at home with your children to instill a love of learning**
● **How to incorporate learning into everyday activities**
● **How to help your children take what they learn at school and apply it to real life situations**

123

You don't need to teach your child all the facts about each and every subject. These activities will help instill in your children a love for the subjects and a curiosity regarding them. Most importantly, by doing these activities at home, your children will have a better understanding of how the subjects they learn at school can be applied to real life situations.

Math Activities:

1. Play math games with your children. Yahtzee™, Battleship™, and Monopoly™ are just a few of the games you can play with your children to increase their understanding of mathematical concepts. Chess and checkers are good games to teach strategy. Dominoes and card games like *Go Fish* and *War* help kids learn about numbers, comparisons, and patterns.
2. Find household items that need sorting. Buttons, socks, coins, stones, etc., can be used. A fun activity is to take an empty egg carton and a group of unassorted items. Ask your children to sort them. When they are finished ask them to explain how they sorted them. Then ask them to sort them another way. Again ask how they sorted them.

Kids First!

3. In the kitchen. There are many ways to increase your children's mathematical skills in the kitchen:
● Use beans, cereal, or any other small item as math manipulatives. These can be used for counting, adding, subtracting, multiplying, etc. A fun activity is to make counting sticks. Take 10 popsicle sticks and glue ten kidney beans onto each one. Your children can use these to add, subtract, and count by tens.
● When cooking, invite your children to do the measuring for you. Talk about fractions like 1/2 cup, 1/4 teaspoon, etc.
● Cut foods like pizza into fractions. Ask your children what fraction of the pizza they are eating.
● Cut sandwiches into different shapes. Discuss the shapes with your child.
4. When shopping for food, allow your children to take calculators and add up the cost of the items. Also allow them to use coupons and figure savings. For younger children, ask them how many things they can buy with a dollar? Let them add up the items to figure out the cost. Let your children pay for something with a dollar and count the change.
5. On family vacations allow your children to compute mileage and the cost of gas for the trip. Even let them do a budget for the trip if they want.

Module 9:
Learning
Is Fun!
Activities
Parents Can
Do To Instill
A Love Of
Learning

Math
Activities

Module 9:
Learning
Is Fun!
Activities
Parents Can
Do To Instill
A Love Of
Learning

Math
Activities

6. Open a savings and checking account for your children. Show them how to balance a checkbook and save for the things they want to buy.

7. Use the newspaper to discuss math concepts. The sports, weather, and stock market pages provide excellent opportunities to discuss number and money concepts with your children.

8. Play the money game. You need: a die, 10 of each coin (penny, nickel, dime), and 6 quarters. For young players (5-6 year olds) use only 2 different coins (pennies and nickels or nickels and dimes). Explain that the object of the game is to be the first player to earn a set amount of money (10 to 30 cents is a good amount). Each player rolls the die and gets the number of pennies shown. As each player accumulates 5 pennies or more, the 5 pennies are traded for a nickel. The first player who reaches the set amount wins.

9. Keep a jar and save all your pennies. Tell your children they can spend them if they can figure out how to count them. Give them plastic baggies or get coin wrappers from the bank and show them how to package them.

10. Talk about time. Let your children time how long it takes to take a bath, get ready for bed, make breakfast, etc.

11. Make flashcards to study math addition, subtraction, multiplication or division facts.

12. Make up songs to favorite tunes to study math facts or buy tapes at teacher supplies stores with math fact songs.

 Science Activities:

You don't need to teach your children all the facts about science. What you want to teach them is a love and curiosity for it.

1. Discuss scientific discoveries and scientists.
2. Check out books at the library on science. Joanna Cole's *Magic School Bus* books are favorite's of many children.
3. Use the backyard, family trips, and newspapers to talk about science.
4. Go to science museums.
5. Watch scientific television programs.
6. Rent scientific videos from the video store.
7. Subscribe to science magazines like *National Geographic World*.

Module 9:
Learning
Is Fun!
Activities
Parents Can
Do To Instill
A Love Of
Learning

Science
Activities

More Science Activities:

1. Collect rocks. Check out a book on rocks at the library and determine the type of rocks you collected.

2. Graph the weather. Make a chart with the following words down one side: Sunny, Cloudy, Rainy, Overcast, Foggy. Every day for a month have your children put a star by the kind of weather it is in the morning. Your children can check the daily weather report in the newspaper if they want it to be more accurate.

3. Make a rain collector. You'll need a plastic bottle and a funnel. Put the funnel in the bottle and place it outside. Collect rain and measure how many inches it rains in one month.

4. Plants are the only things on earth that turn sunlight into food. They do it through a process called photosynthesis. Children can learn about photosynthesis by taking a shoe box and cutting a 1 inch by 2 inch rectangle in one side of the lid. Then fill the box with dirt and plant 3-4 small green plants. Put the lid on the box and wait a few days. The plants should have all grown toward the light.

5. Teach children about colors by taking white cake frosting and food coloring and mixing a tablespoon of frosting with red, yellow, and blue food

Module 9:
Learning
Is Fun!
Activities
Parents Can
Do To Instill
A Love Of
Learning

Science
Activities

coloring. Mix the red and yellow frosting together. What color does it make? Mix the yellow and blue together. What color does it make? Mix the red and blue together. What color does it make? Put the frosting on Graham crackers when finished and eat.

6. Study the stars at night. Point out the different constellations. Discuss the planets and the sun.
7. Save knick-knacks that you would usually throw away in a shoe box. After you have accumulated about ten items, give the box to your children and let them be inventors. Tell them to use their imaginations to make unique inventions. You may want to check out books at the library on famous inventors and their inventions to discuss with your children beforehand. You'll be surprised at their creativity.

History Activities:

1. Make a family tree with your children. Discuss the history of your family.
2. When celebrating holidays, discuss the importance of the person or day being recognized, i.e., Thanksgiving, Lincoln and Washington's Birthdays.

Module 9:
Learning
Is Fun!
Activities
Parents Can
Do To Instill
A Love Of
Learning

History
Activities

3. Get to know the history of your community and country. Visit local landmarks and visit historical sites in our country when on vacation.

4. Encourage your children to read historical fiction and non-fiction.

5. Watch historical biographies with your children on TV.

6. Make timelines with your children. Make them for their favorite historical time periods, historical hero, and for their own lives.

7. Have your children do a pretend interview with a historical figure. Have them list ten questions they would like to ask that person and ten answers that person would give. If they like, they can make a pretend interview on an audio tape using a different voice when answering for the historical figure.

8. Interview on audio or video tape a grandparent. Ask her about her life. What exciting things happened to her? Places she's lived, jobs she's had, etc.

9. Share family heirlooms with your children and discuss their significance.

10. Share family traditions with your children.

Geography Activities:

1. Get a world map and some push pins. Choose an international story to follow in the news or newspaper. Talk about the geographic area. Get books, recipes, etc., on that area.

2. Make a topography map showing the continents of the world or a specific country. Use the following recipe to make the clay:

   > In a large bowl combine the following:
   > 2 1/2 cups of all-purpose flour
   > 1 cup of salt
   > 1 cup of water

   Mold the clay onto a cardboard or wood surface and let dry overnight. Paint it the next day.

3. Discuss the characteristics of the different continents.

4. Subscribe to magazines like *Discover, World, Ranger Rick* and *Your Big Backyard.*

5. Do puzzles of maps.

6. Make different ethnic recipes and discuss the countries they come from.

7. Read stories at holiday time about places and celebrations around the world.

8. Make a pretend passport and pretend to travel to

different countries.

9. Learn simple words in another language.

10. Invite friends that have traveled over to share their pictures and slides.

Module 9:
Learning
Is Fun!
Activities
Parents Can
Do To Instill
A Love Of
Learning

Spelling
Activities

Spelling Activities:

1. Use see, say, and write spelling. Take a piece of paper and fold it in half horizontally. Fold it in half again. You should end up with four columns. Have your child first look at the word. Then say it. Then spell it outloud placing a dot under each letter with a pen or pencil. Then your child should cover the word and try to spell it without looking. Your child should then check the word for mistakes and write it correctly in the last column.

2. Play Scrabble™.

3. Get shaving cream and write the spelling words in it on a table.

4. Take the lid of a shoebox or a metal pan. Fill it with salt or sand. Have your children write their spelling words in the sand or salt.

5. Give your children big pieces of washable chalk. Have them write their spelling words in the street.

6. Teach these easy spelling rules (rules apply 80% of the time):

a. Some words double the final consonant when adding a suffix that begins with a vowel.

Get + ing = get + t + ing = getting

big + er = big + g+ er = bigger

b. Some words drop the final e when adding a suffix that begins with a vowel.

have + ing = hav + ing = having

write + ing + writ + ing + writing

c. Some words change y to i when adding a suffix not beginning with i.

Try + ed = tri + ed = tried

try + ing = trying

d. Most nouns form the plural by adding s.

word + s = words

key + s = keys

e. Nouns ending with s, ss, sh, ch, and x form the plural by adding es.

inch + es = inches

class + es = classes

f. Some nouns form the plural by changing f or fe to v when adding es.

half + es = halv + es = halves   wife + es = wiv + es + wives

Module 9:
Learning
Is Fun!
Activities
Parents Can
Do To Instill
A Love Of
Learning

Spelling
Activities

Writing Activities:

Module 9:
Learning
Is Fun!
Activities
Parents Can
Do To Instill
A Love Of
Learning

Writing
Activities

1. Make and write birthday and greeting cards.
2. Make books. Take a shoebox and fill it with scraps of material, paper, crayons, ribbons, glue, scissors, etc. Let your children make books using the materials
3. Write down things around the house. Shopping lists, notes, etc.
4. Write letters to people. Find a pen pal. Write the president, sports heroes, or an organization that represents a specific cause for the environment, etc.
5. Get your children a dictionary.
6. Teach your children the writing process:

    Brainstorm

    Pre-Composing

    Rough Draft

    Reading

    Editing

    Rewriting

    Publishing

7. Teach older children the fundamentals of essay writing. Essays require research, so assist your children in finding books on the subject either from the classroom text, the school library, or the public library.

Kids First!

Use These Easy Steps To Help Teach Children Essay Writing Skills:

1. To begin an essay, start with an introductory paragraph. A good way to structure it is like an inverted triangle. Start with a general statement followed by more specific statements. The last sentence should state exactly what the essay will cover (the thesis statement).
2. The paragraphs that follow should begin with topic sentences that prove or describe the main idea (thesis statement) of the essay.
3. The last paragraph should be a conclusion restating the main idea of the essay.
4. A sample outline of an essay would like this:

Outline

I. Topic: _____

II. Introductory paragraph

   a. General statements (sentences) about the topic
   b. Specific sentence about what will be discussed or proven in the essay (thesis statement).

III. Topic sentences - each one needs to directly relate to the main point (thesis statement) of the essay. 2 -3 topic sentences (each one begins its own paragraph)

   a. Main point to support the topic sentences.
   This should include facts and figures that prove

Module 9:
Learning
Is Fun!
Activities
Parents Can
Do To Instill
A Love Of
Learning

Writing
Activities

Use These
Easy Steps
To Help
Teach
Children
Essay Writing
Skills

your topic sentences.

IV. Conclusion

 You have successfully completed Kids First!™ Family Education Program. Please complete the award certificate on the following page.

Kids First™ Certificate of Completion

awarded to:

_____

Date:_____

Building Our Children's Futures Together!

OTHER TITLES FROM BLUE BIRD PUBLISHING

Available in bookstores and libraries.

Home Schools: An Alternative (4th ed)   *$12.95*
   A home schooling bestseller.

Home Education Resource Guide (4th e.) *$12.95*
   A home schooling bestseller.

Heartful Parenting   *$14.95*
   Discover the secret ingredient to successful parenting.

Dr. Christman's Learn-to-Read Book   *$15.95*
   Phonics program for all ages. Adopted by many
   literacy and right-to-read groups

Kindergarten at Home   *$22.95*
   An interactive kindergarten curriculum for
   homeschoolers. Useful activities for teachers too.

ADD to Excellent Without Drugs   *$12.95*
   A non-drug approach to helping children and adults
   with ADD/ADHD.

Kids First! Family Education Program   *$12.95*
   Gets parents involved in their child's education.

Blue Bird Publishing
2266 S. Dobson #275
Mesa AZ 85202
(602) 831-6063 FAX (602) 831-1829
Email: bluebird@bluebird1.com
Web Site: www.bluebird1.com